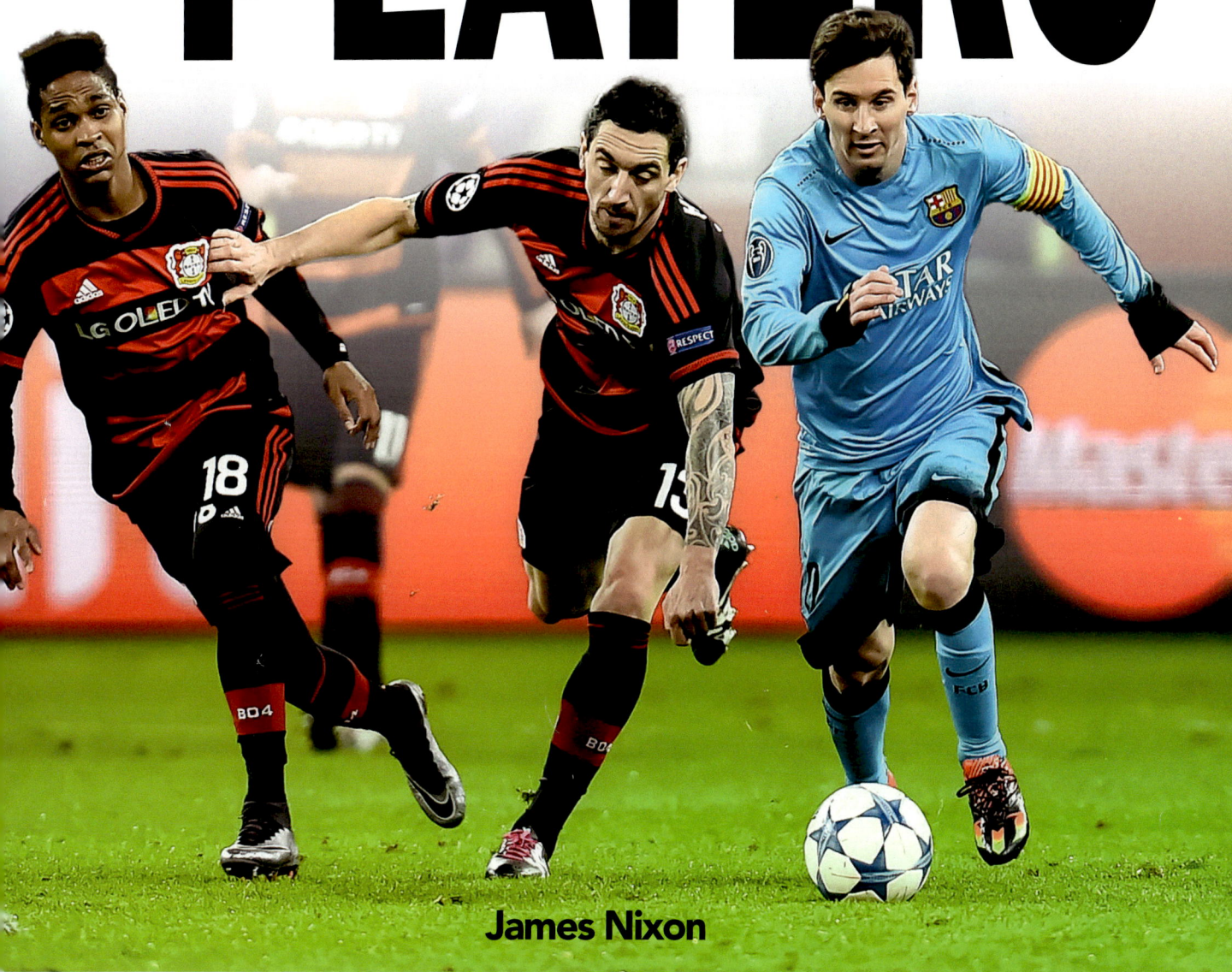

FOOTBALL WORLD

PLAYERS

James Nixon

W

FRANKLIN WATTS

LONDON • SYDNEY

Franklin Watts
First published in Great Britain in 2017 by The Watts Publishing Group

Credits
Editor: James Nixon
Design: Keith Williams, sprout.uk.com
Planning and production by Discovery Books Limited

Photo credits: Cover image: Alamy (GUIDO KIRCHNER/dpa).
Bigstock: pp. 4 (Maxisports), 8 bottom (Celso Pupo), 10 top (sportsphotographer.eu), 11 top (Celso Pupo), 12 middle (Maxisports), 12 bottom (bettorodrigues), 13 top and bottom (sportsphotographer.eu), 14 bottom (vverve), 15 top (Celso Pupo), 15 bottom (katatonia82), 16 top (Maxisports), 17 top (Maxisports), 18 bottom (Maxisports), 20 top (Maxisports), 21 top (Celso Pupo), 21 bottom (hkratky), 23 bottom (katatonia82), 24 top (sportsphotographer.eu) 25 bottom (Celso Pupo), 29 top (sportsphotographer.eu), 31 (katatonia82).
Getty Images: 5 bottom (Dan Mullan/Stringer), 6 top (Manuel Queimadelos Alonso/Stringer), 9 bottom (JEFF PACHOUD/AFP), 14 top (Alex Broadway/Stringer), 19 top (Catherine Ivill – AMA), 19 bottom (Hector Vivas/STR), 22 bottom (Clive Brunskill), 24 bottom (John Peters), 25 top (GLYN KIRK/AFP).
Shutterstock: pp. 5 top (Marcos Mesa Sam Wordley), 6 bottom (Vlad1988), 7 top (Cristiano Barni), 8 top (imagestockdesign), 9 top (MediaPictures.pl), 10 bottom (CosminIftode), 11 bottom (Fingerhut), 12 top (Marco Iacobucci EPP), 16 bottom (Vlad1988), 17 bottom (Marco Iacobucci EPP), 18 top (Marco Iacobucci EPP), 20 bottom (CosminIftode), 22 top (AGIF), 23 top (Natursports), 28 top-left (mr3002), 28 top-right (Mitch Gunn).
Wikimedia: pp. 7 bottom (Clément Bucco-Lechat), 26 top (Agência Brasil Fotografias), 26 bottom (Chris Simpson), 27 top (joshjdss), 27 bottom (Pierre-Yves Beaudouin/Wikimedia Commons/CC BY-SA 3.0), 28 bottom (Agência Brasília), 29 bottom (Chensiyuan).

Every attempt has been made to clear copyright. Should there be any inadvertent omission please apply to the publisher for rectification.

HB ISBN: 978 1 4451 5576 0
PB ISBN: 978 1 4451 5577 7

Printed in China

MIX
Paper from responsible sources
FSC
www.fsc.org
FSC® C104740

Franklin Watts
An imprint of
Hachette Children's Group
Part of The Watts Publishing Group
Carmelite House
50 Victoria Embankment
London EC4Y 0DZ

An Hachette UK Company
www.hachette.co.uk

www.franklinwatts.co.uk

The statistics in this book were correct at the time of printing, but because of the nature of sport, it cannot be guaranteed that they are now accurate.

Every effort has been made by the Publishers to ensure that the websites in this book are suitable for children, that they are of the highest educational value, and that they contain no inappropriate or offensive material. However, because of the nature of the Internet, it is impossible to guarantee that the contents of these sites will not be altered. We strongly advise that Internet access is supervised by a responsible adult.

CONTENTS

STARS OF THE GAME

The top footballers in the game come from all over the world. They display their talents while playing for the biggest clubs in Europe's major leagues. Some of today's footballers are so skilful that they can be placed among the greatest in the history of football.

Marvellous Messi

Lionel Messi from Argentina is definitely one of the all-time greats. There is no sight more terrifying to a defender than Messi dribbling at them at full speed. Messi is short for a footballer at just 1.7 metres high. Yet his low **centre of gravity**, plus his quick feet, let him twist, turn and dart past defenders. With his precise passing and finishing, Messi creates and scores an astonishing number of goals.

Messi's skills have helped Spanish club Barcelona become the most successful team in the world in recent years. The Ballon d'Or award, given to the best player in European football, has been won by Messi five times in the last eight years.

FLASH FACT

Lionel Messi holds the record for the most goals scored in a football season (82) and a calendar year (91).

⚽ Stat Tracker

	Games played	Goals
Lionel Messi Barcelona Argentina	555 116	480 57
Cristiano Ronaldo Real Madrid Portugal	368 136	381 68
Gareth Bale Real Madrid Wales	139 65	65 26

Cristiano Ronaldo

Messi's main challenger for the Ballon d'Or has been Portugal's captain Cristiano Ronaldo, with Ronaldo winning the award four times including in 2016. Ronaldo plays for Barcelona's major rivals in Spain, Real Madrid. Ronaldo is a much bigger, stronger player than Messi but equally fast, skilful and deadly in front of goal. Ronaldo uses his great leap to score lots of headers. He holds the record for the most goals in a Champions League season (17) and is the only player to score over 50 goals in a season six times running. In 2016, it was reported that Ronaldo was the world's highest-paid athlete.

Welsh wizard

Gareth Bale is the biggest footballing superstar from the UK. The Welsh winger can dribble past his opponents with blistering pace and has a wicked, swerving shot. Real Madrid signed Bale from Tottenham Hotspur in 2013 for what was then a world record fee of £85 million!

SKILL PLAYERS

The most skilled footballers can get the crowd in the stadium out of their seats. They can mesmerise defenders with their dribbles and skills. These players are difference-makers – in an instant they can turn a game heading for a 0-0 draw into victory for their team.

Neymar

Brazilian captain Neymar is another star in Barcelona's amazing forward line. Known for his dribbling, finishing and ability with both feet, Neymar's performances are extraordinary and hugely entertaining. He has all the tricks in the book, from **dummies** and **stepovers** to fool defenders, to backheels and flicks that create chances for his teammates. Neymar is still young enough to become the best player in the world. In 2016, he scored the winning **penalty** to earn Brazil the Olympic gold medal.

FLASH FACT

In 2015, Neymar and Lionel Messi helped Barcelona score 180 goals in total, setting the record for the most goals scored by a team in one calendar year.

Watch out – Hazard!

Belgium and Chelsea forward Eden Hazard is probably the most dangerous attacker in the Premier League when running at defenders. Hazard's close control at pace makes it often appear as if the ball is glued to his foot. This lets him go past his opponent in even the tightest of spots.

Free kick king

Bosnian midfielder Miralem Pjanić is one of the most technically gifted footballers in the world. His quick feet, close control and clever touches are a joy to watch. Dubbed the 'Little Prince', Pjanić was signed by Italian giants Juventus in 2016. Pjanić is also considered by some to be the world's best free-kick taker. He is able to curl the ball over a defensive wall and into the net with incredible accuracy.

Stat Tracker

	Games played	Goals
Neymar		
Barcelona	162	92
Brazil	75	50
Eden Hazard		
Chelsea	228	62
Belgium	76	17
Miralem Pjanić		
Juventus	18	6
Bosnia	72	11
Yacine Brahimi		
Porto	99	25
Algeria	31	7

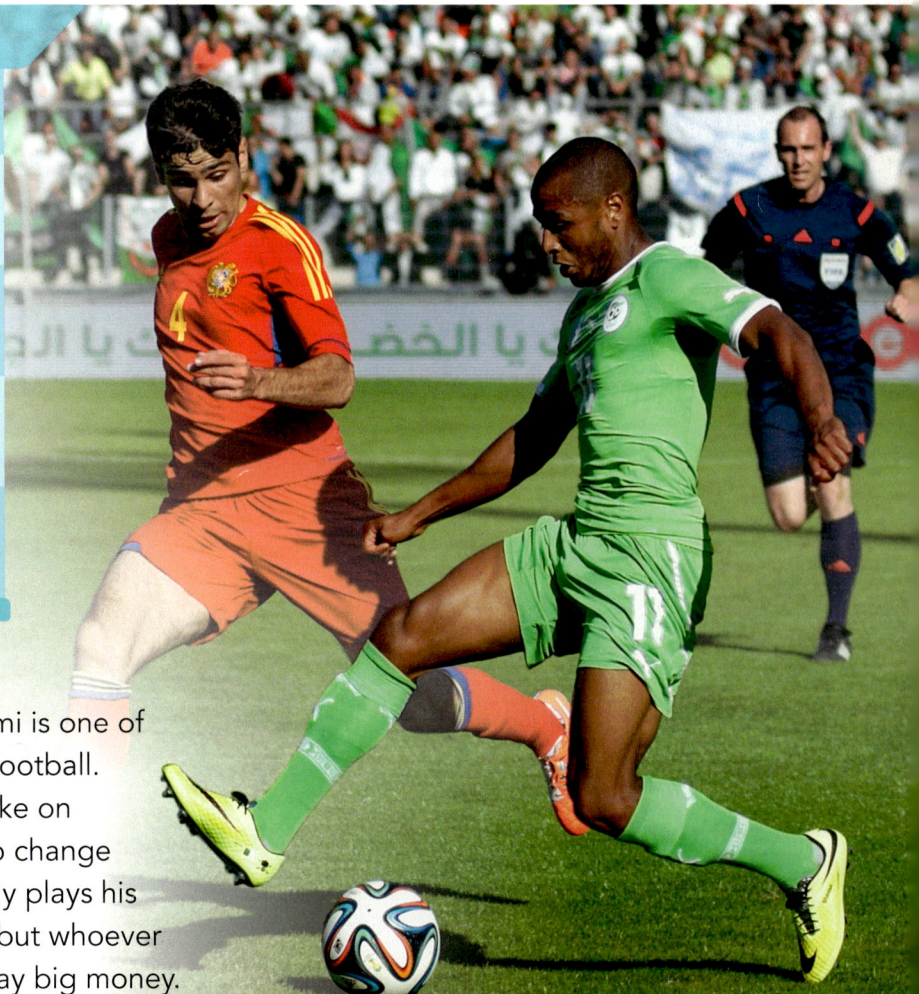

Yacine Brahimi

Algerian international Yacine Brahimi is one of the most exciting players in world football. Brahimi just loves to dribble and take on players, using his tricks and pace to change direction in a flash. Brahimi currently plays his club football for Porto in Portugal, but whoever signs him next will surely have to pay big money.

PURE GOALSCORERS

Goals win football matches, so high-scoring strikers are in demand. The very best finishers keep cool in that moment of pressure and are deadly accurate.

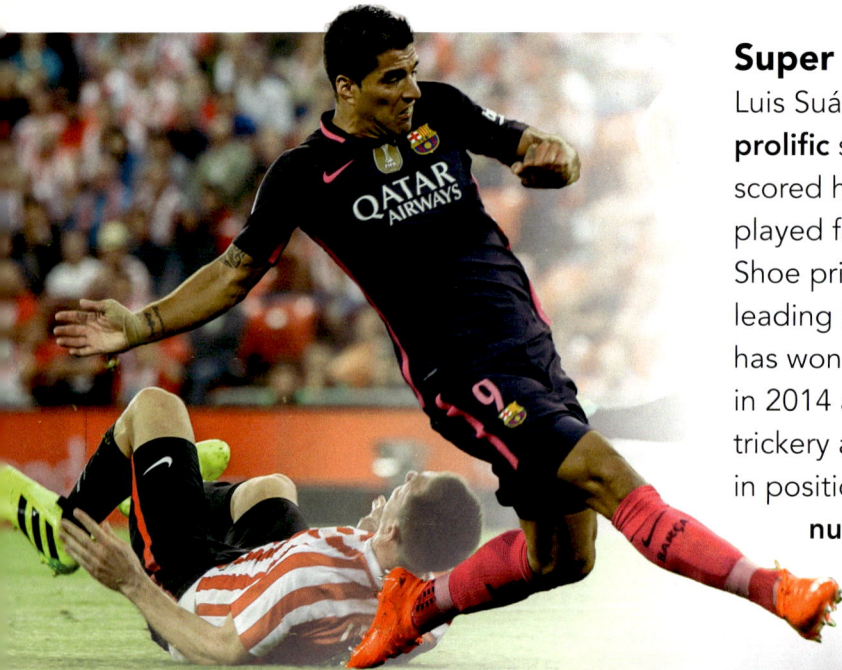

Super Suárez

Luis Suárez from Uruguay is one of the most **prolific** strikers in football history. He has scored heaps of goals at all the clubs he has played for. The European Golden Shoe prize is given to Europe's leading league goalscorer. Suárez has won this twice, while at Liverpool in 2014 and at Barcelona in 2016. His trickery and direct running often put Suárez in positions to score. His favourite move is to **nutmeg** the defender to get past them.

Sergio Agüero

Argentina and Manchester City striker Sergio Agüero can terrorise defenders like few others. Agüero has one of the highest goals-per-minute ratio in the history of the Premier League. His razor-sharp movement and supreme strength and balance can leave opponents for dead. Agüero can strike the ball powerfully with both feet and can finish well from inside and outside the penalty box.

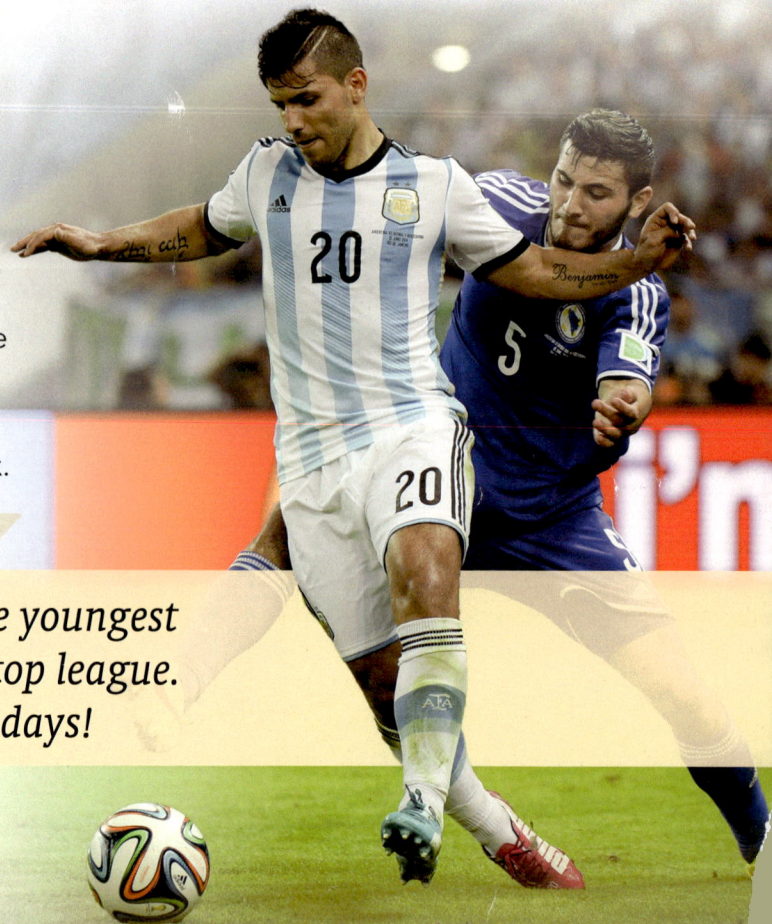

FLASH FACT

In 2003, Sergio Agüero became the youngest player to compete in Argentina's top league. He was aged just 15 years and 35 days!

Robert Lewandowski

Poland captain Robert Lewandowski is one of today's most impressive finishers. Starring for Bayern Munich in the 2015/16 season, he ended up as the Bundesliga's top scorer, netting 30 times in 32 appearances. Amazingly, with his side 1-0 down to Wolfsburg, Lewandowski came on as substitute and scored five goals in the space of nine minutes! For this achievement Lewandowski was awarded four different Guiness World Records!

Alexandre Lacazette

French striker Alexandre Lacazette has been in sensational form for his club Lyon. In 2015, he scored 27 goals in 33 appearances to finish top scorer in the French top division. He was also named the league's Player of the Year. Like all good strikers, Lacazette can score all types of goals, whether it is **one-on-ones**, volleys or long shots.

Stat Tracker

	Games played	Goals
Luis Suárez Barcelona Uruguay	121 90	102 47
Sergio Agüero Manchester City Argentina	230 80	154 33
Robert Lewandowski Bayern Munich Poland	124 85	87 42
Alexandre Lacazette Lyon France	251 10	108 1

TARGETMEN

As well as scoring goals, strikers that play as targetmen have the job of winning long balls and holding on to the ball while their teammates advance up the pitch. Each of these four players make perfect targets.

Diego Costa

Spanish striker Diego Costa doesn't give defenders a moment's peace. His determination and willingness to chase down long balls puts the opposition under pressure. Costa is also extremely strong, which means he is expert at battling for the ball and holding on to **possession**. But best of all, he is a natural finisher. He helped Atlético Madrid win a Spanish league title in 2014 before winning the Premier League with Chelsea in 2015.

Harry Kane

This England and Tottenham Hotspur striker has all the skills needed to be a top targetman. He is tall so he can challenge for long aerial balls, but he also has good technique, so he can control passes to his feet and hold on to the ball while he is being marked. Kane's pace is decent too, which allows him to run on to balls played behind the defence. His powerful and accurate shooting helped him win the Premier League **Golden Boot** in 2016.

FLASH FACT

*In 2015, Harry Kane made his England **debut** against Lithuania and scored with a header after just 80 seconds!*

Romelu Lukaku

Everton and Belgium international Romelu Lukaku is the classic big and strong targetman. With his back to defenders, he has the ability to use his muscle to spin away from them towards goal. Many of Lukaku's goals are headers from crosses. Lukaku is one of only five players in history to score 50 Premier League goals before his 23rd birthday.

Stat Tracker

	Games played	Goals
Diego Costa Chelsea Spain	99 14	51 4
Harry Kane Tottenham Hotspur England	146 17	79 5
Romelu Lukaku Everton Belgium	148 54	73 19
Pierre-Emerick Aubameyang Borussia Dortmund Gabon	165 53	100 22

African star

Pierre-Emerick Aubameyang is one of the most dangerous strikers in world football. He plays for the Gabon national team and Borussia Dortmund in Germany. Known for his electric speed, he can beat defenders to long passes over the top and through the back line. In the 2015/16 season he scored 39 goals in 46 games for Dortmund and was awarded Bundesliga Player of the Year and African Footballer of the Year.

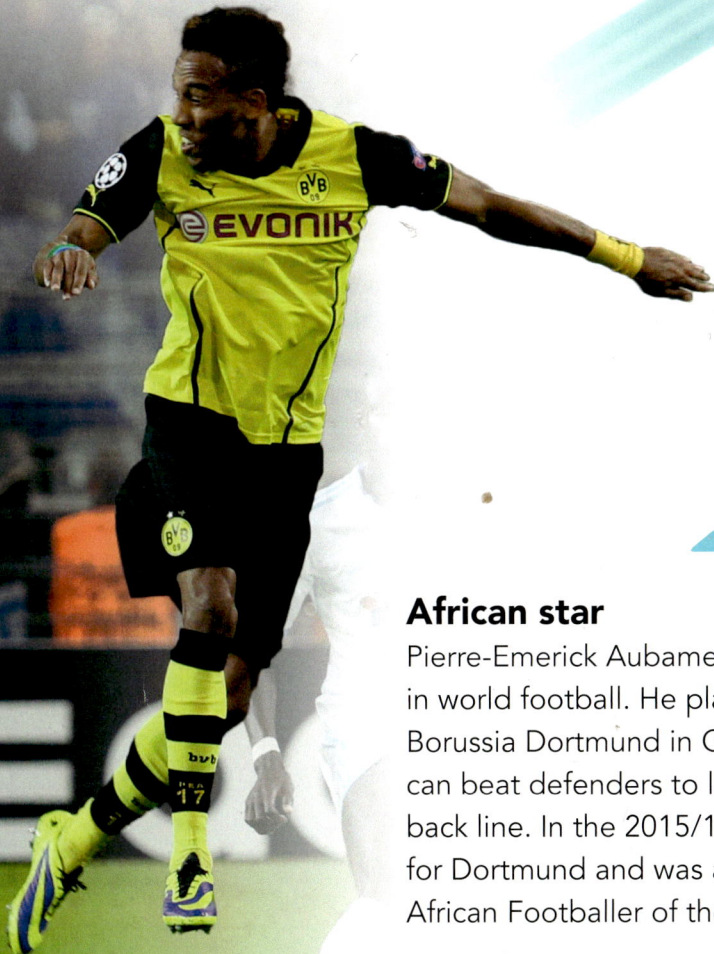

NUMBER TENS

The number ten shirt is often worn by the deeper-lying support striker or the central attacking midfielder. 'Number ten' has since become the name for this position between midfield and attack. The job of a number ten is to create goals as well as score them.

Kevin De Bruyne

Arguably the best player in the Premier League, Belgian Kevin De Bruyne is a master in the number ten role. He was signed by Manchester City in 2015 for a club record £55 million. De Bruyne **assists** many goals with his intelligent and pinpoint passing that can split open defences. He scores plenty too, including some stunning strikes from outside the box.

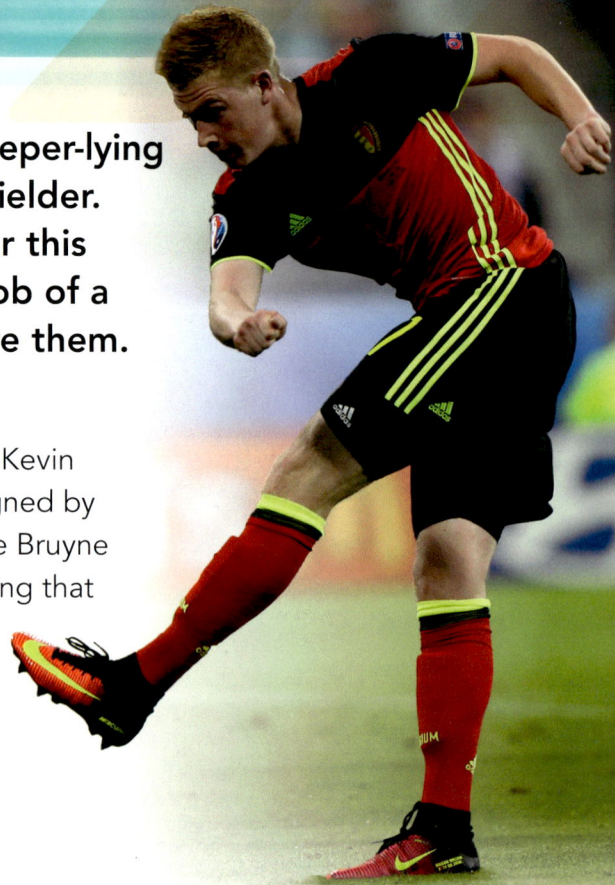

Star of the Euros

Antoine Griezmann has been a scoring sensation for France and his Spanish club Atlético Madrid. At Euro 2016 Griezmann was the top scorer and named Player of the Tournament. Griezmann is an all-round talent. He has pace, energy, clever movement and can link up play between the midfielders and attackers. On top of this, he takes **set pieces** and penalties and can finish well with both feet and his head.

FLASH FACT

The Golden Boot winner at the 2014 World Cup was Colombian and Real Madrid number ten James Rodríguez. He scored six goals in five games.

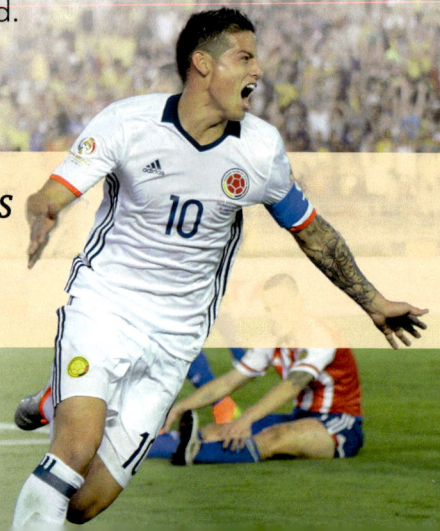

Thomas Müller

Number tens can be hard for opponents to mark because they drift about in that space between midfield and attack. There is no greater example of this than Bayern Munich and German forward Thomas Müller. Müller is not the most amazingly skilful player, yet he consistently scores and creates goals. How does he do this? His skill lies in his movement and ability to find space. Then, in front of goal, he is incredibly cool.

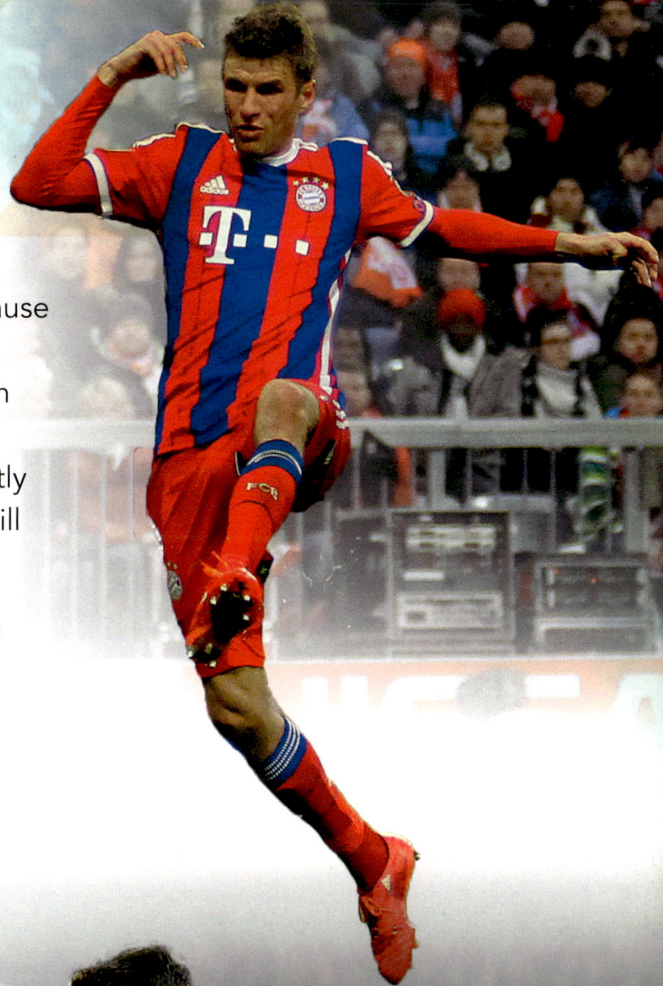

⚽ Stat Tracker

	Games played	Goals
Kevin De Bruyne Manchester City Belgium	66 48	19 12
Antoine Griezmann Atlético Madrid France	132 39	69 14
Thomas Müller Bayern Munich Germany	375 83	156 36
Mesut Özil Arsenal Germany	140 83	29 21

Assist king

Müller's German teammate Mesut Özil can also play the number ten role. The Arsenal star is a genius and creates goalscoring chance after chance with his **vision**, imagination and crossing ability. He sees passes that other players wouldn't. Sometimes called the assist king, Özil has the highest ratio of assists per game in the history of the Premier League.

TRICKY WINGERS

Wingers play and attack down the sides of the pitch. The best wingers use pace and trickery to get past their opponents and can deliver dangerous crosses into the box.

Riyad Mahrez

Algerian winger Riyad Mahrez played a key role in Leicester City's shock Premier League win in 2016. Before the season, Leicester were given a one in 5,000 chance of winning! Mahrez ended up being voted the **PFA** Player's Player of the Year. Dribbling mainly with his left foot, Mahrez can effortlessly dodge past defenders. His lethal, curling shots added 17 goals to Leicester's victory tally, easily more than any other non-striker in the league.

Stat Tracker

	Games played	Goals
Riyad Mahrez Leicester City Algeria	116 27	32 6
Douglas Costa Bayern Munich Brazil	59 19	11 3
Alexis Sánchez Arsenal Chile	121 106	58 36
Raheem Sterling Manchester City England	73 29	17 2

Douglas Costa

Brazilian Douglas Costa joined Bayern Munich for €30 million in 2015. Costa has loads of pace and his dazzling dribbling and wicked crosses terrify defences. Costa can play on either wing. He can dribble down the outside on the left or cut inside from the right and unleash his powerful left-foot shot.

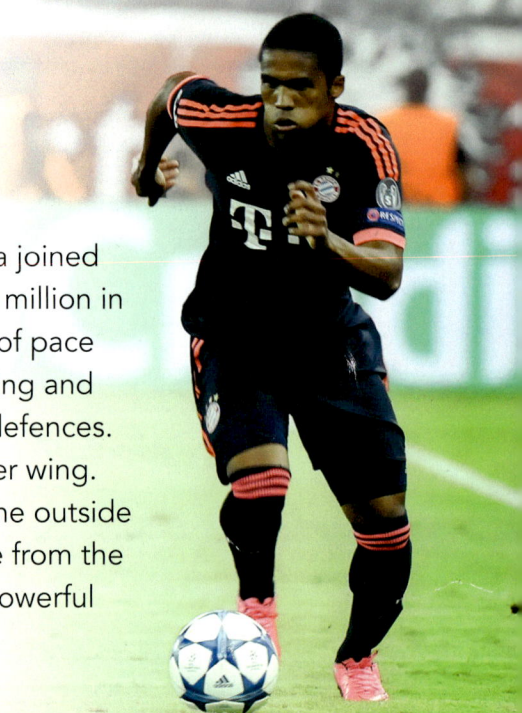

Alexis Sánchez

Arsenal winger Alexis Sánchez (left) has helped his nation Chile win the last two **Copa America** championships and in 2016 he was awarded the Golden Ball as the tournament's best player. Quick, agile, and with huge amounts of flair, Sánchez can skip past opponents. Like many top wingers, Sánchez has the **work rate** and energy to track back and help his defence, too.

FLASH FACT

*In Chile's 2016 Copa America semi-final victory over Colombia, Alexis Sánchez became the first Chilean outfield player to reach 100 **caps**.*

Raheem Sterling

Manchester City signed winger Raheem Sterling from Liverpool for £49 million in 2015. This was the highest **transfer** fee ever paid for an English player. The year before he had won the Golden Boy award given to the best under-21 player in Europe. Sterling is a small, pacy winger who has the craft and dribbling skills to unlock any defence.

PASS MASTERS

A team can't score if they don't have the ball. Keeping possession and accurate passing is key to winning football matches. Here are some of the top players that make their teams tick.

Toni Kroos

German and Real Madrid midfielder Toni Kroos is known for his phenomenal passing accuracy. In 2014, Kroos won the prize for the World's Best Playmaker awarded by the International Federation of Football History and Statistics (IFFHS). Playmakers like Kroos are fluent in receiving and passing the ball and make the game look easy. Kroos also sets up many goals with his superb vision and set pieces. He recorded the highest number of assists in the 2014 World Cup to help Germany win the trophy.

FLASH FACT

*In 2014, Toni Kroos became the first player born in the former country of **East Germany** to win a World Cup.*

Mini maestro

Italian international Marco Verratti stands at just 1.65 metres tall, yet he is one of the finest midfielders in the world. Verratti is super-confident on the ball and very rarely gives it away. His close ball control and low centre of gravity help him hold on to possession in tight spaces. Verratti controls the tempo of his side's play. He is a master of long and short passing and can play a killer final pass to the strikers too. Since he joined French club Paris Saint-Germain in 2012, his team have won four French league titles in a row.

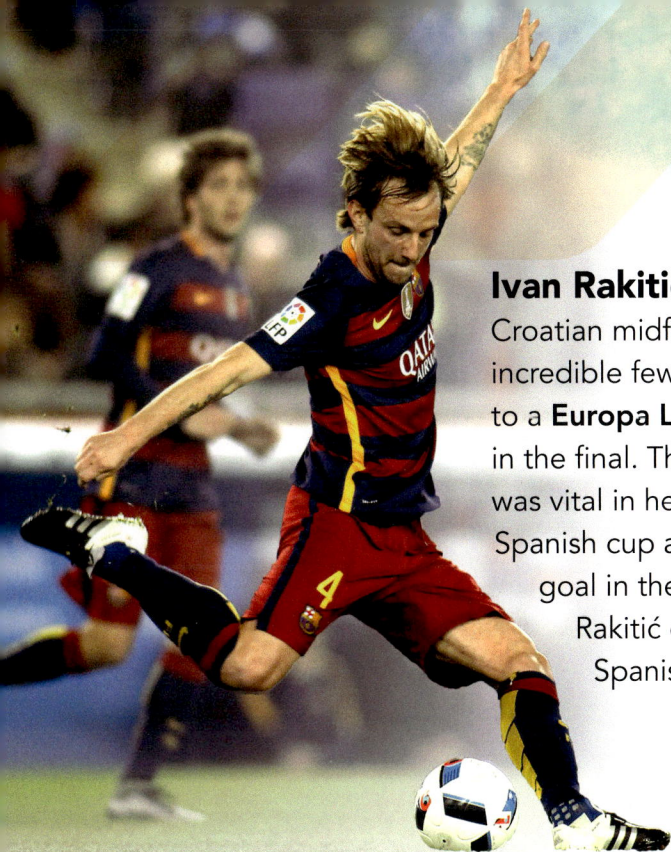

Ivan Rakitić

Croatian midfielder and playmaker Ivan Rakitić has had an incredible few years. In 2014, he captained Spanish club Sevilla to a **Europa League** triumph and was named Man of the Match in the final. This earned Rakitić a move to Barcelona where he was vital in helping the team win a 2015 treble (Spanish league, Spanish cup and Champions League). He scored the opening goal in the 3-1 Champions League final win over Juventus. Rakitić continued to shine in 2016 as Barcelona won the Spanish league and cup again.

Leonardo Bonucci

It is not just midfielders that need to be good at passing. Italian defender Leonardo Bonucci is expert at directing play from the back with precise passing. Bonucci is a cool defender who doesn't panic with the ball at his feet. In fact he has the ability to launch attacks with his long passes. Bonucci has helped Juventus win five Italian league championships in a row!

⚽ Stat Tracker

	Games played	Goals
Toni Kroos Real Madrid Germany	122 74	4 12
Marco Verratti Paris Saint-Germain Italy	180 19	5 1
Ivan Rakitić Barcelona Croatia	131 81	20 13
Leonardo Bonucci Juventus Italy	290 67	18 4

MIDFIELD DESTROYERS

Successful teams more often than not win the midfield battle. They have midfielders that are energetic, strong and tough in the tackle. These players protect their team's defence and help to kickstart attacks.

Paul Pogba

French star Paul Pogba is the most expensive footballer in history. Manchester United signed him from Juventus for a record transfer fee of £89 million in 2016. Pogba is a **commanding** midfielder with his tall frame and long legs. He has the stamina and skill of a **box-to-box midfielder**. He will tackle and block shots in defence, but can also power forward into his opponent's box to score. But what sets Pogba apart are his ball skills. The way he can swiftly change the play from defence to attack is something special.

FLASH FACT

Paul Pogba won the Best Young Player award at the 2014 World Cup. The prize is contested between players at the tournament aged 21 or under.

Busy Busquets

Sergio Busquets is the quiet hero of the Spain and Barcelona team. He may not have the flashy skills of the big names, but he is just as important. Busquets is the master of positioning, always in place to **intercept** an attack and shield his defence. And when he wins the ball, he rarely loses possession.

The interceptor

N'Golo Kanté was one of the biggest stars in Leicester City's 2016 Premier League fairytale. Chelsea signed him the following summer for £32 million. Despite measuring just 1.69 metres Kanté is a true midfield destroyer. His tackling is hard and well timed, but he is also expert at breaking down opponents' attacks by making interceptions. The secret to this skill is his ability to read the game, which means he can predict what his opponents will do next. Kanté is also comfortable bursting forward with the ball to put the opposition's defence under pressure.

The warrior

Chilean international Arturo Vidal (below right) is a complete midfielder, known for his tackling, passing and powerful shots from distance. His physical and aggressive style of play earned him the nickname 'The Warrior' when he was at Juventus. Bayern Munich signed Vidal for €37 million in 2015.

⚽ Stat Tracker

	Games played	Goals
Paul Pogba Manchester United France	27 44	6 8
Sergio Busquets Barcelona Spain	409 94	12 2
N'Golo Kanté Chelsea France	21 13	1 1
Arturo Vidal Bayern Munich Chile	68 86	10 20

FLYING FULL BACKS

Full backs play either side of the central defenders. The best full backs are just as skilled in attacking as defending. To sprint up and down the pitch, these players need good pace and stamina.

Jordi Alba

Spain's Jordi Alba is Barcelona's speedy left back. Attacking wingers up against Alba usually find themselves running backwards chasing Alba instead. Alba is skilful enough to play as a winger himself. In 2016, he scored the crucial goal in extra time as Barcelona beat Sevilla to win the Spanish cup.

Speedy Walker

Kyle Walker (below left) is England's top right back. The powerful Spurs player just loves to burst down the right **touchline** and swing crosses into the opposition's box. Defensively he has the pace to track back and make vital tackles. In 2012, Walker was judged to have had the best season in the Premier League among players aged 23 or under. This won him the Young Player of the Year award.

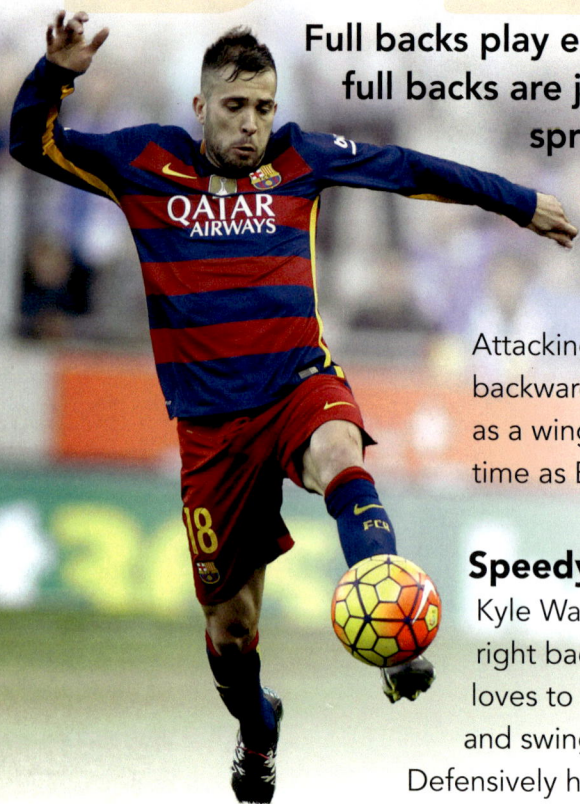

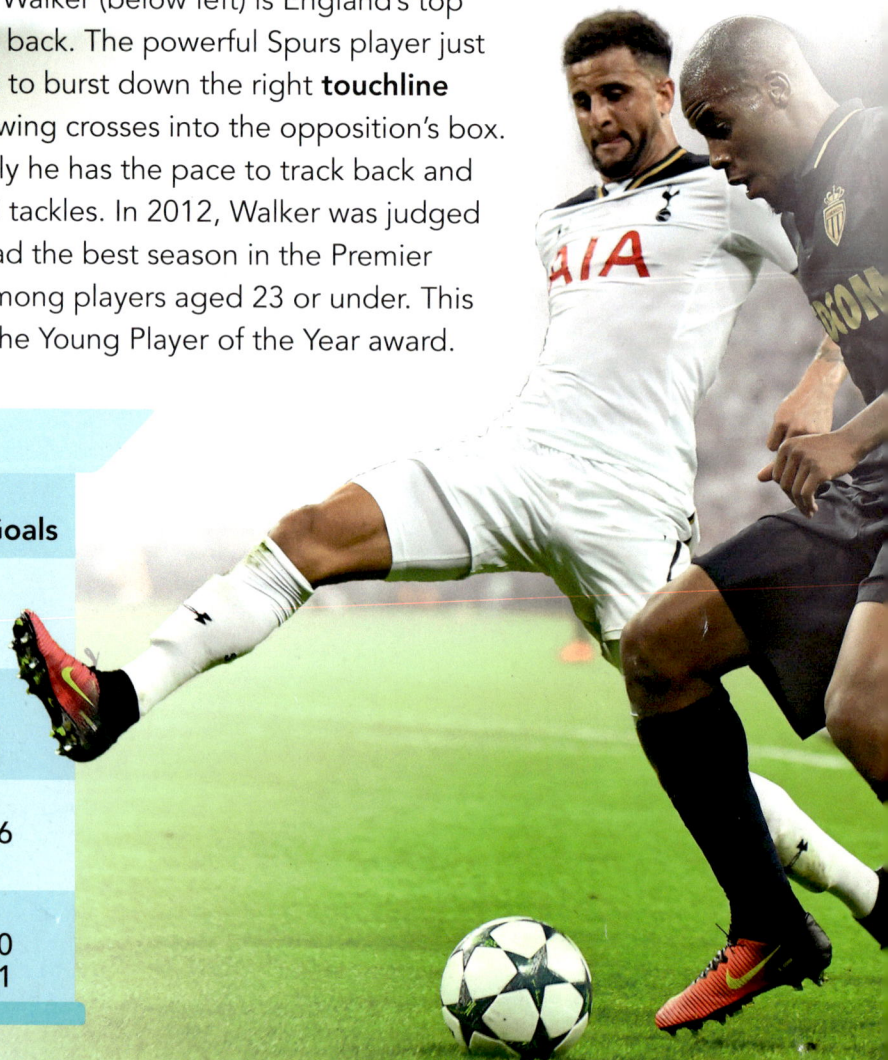

Stat Tracker

	Games played	Goals
Jordi Alba Barcelona Spain	177 50	9 6
Kyle Walker Tottenham Hotspur England	211 23	4 0
Marcelo Real Madrid Brazil	383 45	26 4
David Alaba Bayern Munich Austria	241 50	20 11

Marcelo

Brazilian left back Marcelo is without question the most skilful defender in the world today. Marcelo is able to dribble past player after player, yet he combines this attacking flair with defensive steel. Football legend Diego Maradona commented that the Real Madrid full back was the third best player in the Spanish league after Cristiano Ronaldo and Lionel Messi!

David Alaba

Bayern Munich left back David Alaba has been a revelation for the German champions. Alaba has the quickness to charge into space but also to recover when his team's attack fizzles out. He has such great passing and shooting ability that his country Austria uses Alaba as a number ten and the driving force behind their attacks!

FLASH FACT

David Alaba was Austrian Footballer of the Year five years running between 2011 and 2015 and gained the record of Austria's youngest ever capped player when he was 17.

TOP DEFENDERS

Stopping goals is just as important as scoring them. A defender's job is to block shots, tackle, win headers and mark forwards. Here are some of the best in the business.

A powerhouse

Jérôme Boateng (right) is one of the strongest and toughest defenders in the world. The Bayern Munich and German powerhouse is dominant in the air and makes crunching tackles. His pace helps him close down attackers in a flash. Boateng played a starring role for Germany in their 2014 World Cup final victory. In that game Boateng won 83 per cent of his duels, made loads of tackles, but only committed one **foul** over the entire 120 minutes.

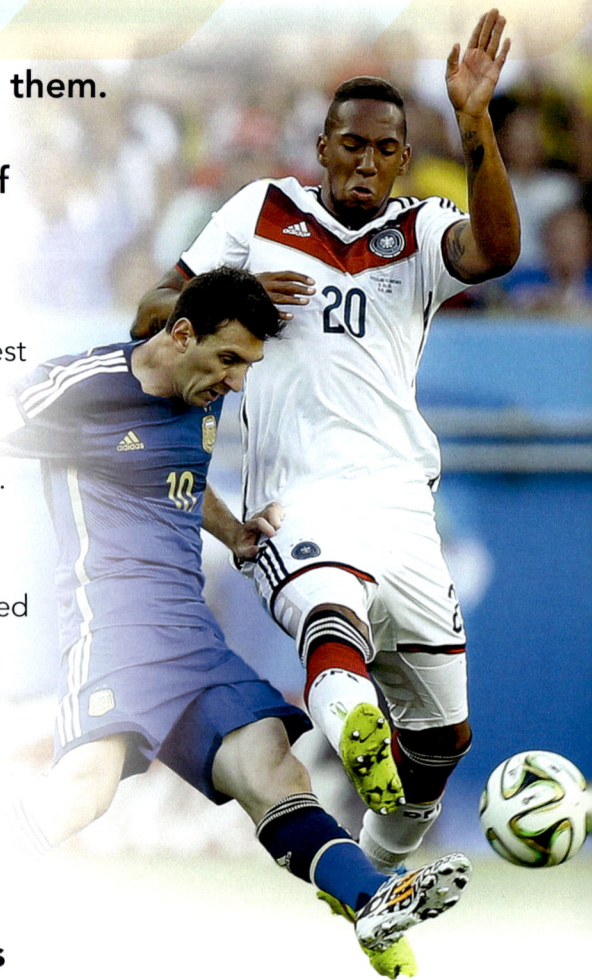

Solid as Stones

In 2016, at the age of 22, England defender John Stones moved from Everton to Manchester City for £47.5 million! Manchester City signed Stones for his calmness and ability to pass and move his way out of danger. Commanding in the air and on the ground, Stones has everything it takes to become one of the game's greats.

FLASH FACT

John Stones' transfer to Manchester City saw him become the second most expensive defender in history, just behind Chelsea's Brazilian centre back David Luiz.

Raphaël Varane

Real Madrid and French defender Raphaël Varane is another youngster with a huge future. At just 23 he reads the game like a **veteran**. Even if he does find himself caught out of position, Varane has the ability to use his searing pace and execute a perfect sliding tackle. Aged 22 he became the youngest player ever to wear the captain's armband for France.

Spanish master

Gerard Piqué (below left) has been another key player in Spain and Barcelona's recent success. Piqué's height and strength combined with good technique and passing has made him one of the game's most solid defenders. Piqué also has the anticipation of a striker in the opponent's box and often pops up with a crucial headed goal.

⚽ Stat Tracker

	Games played	Goals
Jérôme Boateng Bayern Munich Germany	218 67	6 1
John Stones Manchester City England	25 15	1 0
Raphaël Varane Real Madrid France	172 35	10 2
Gerard Piqué Barcelona Spain	376 84	35 5

GOALKEEPERS

The greatest goalkeepers can produce heroic and spellbinding saves to help their teams win any match. These players must be supremely **agile** and athletic.

Sweeper keeper

Bayern Munich goalkeeper Manuel Neuer is regarded as one of the best goalkeepers of all time. Neuer is a fantastic shot-stopper and commands his area well by punching away and catching crosses. He also likes to rush outside his penalty box and beat strikers to the ball. Neuer is a bit like an 11th outfield player spraying pinpoint passes around the pitch. This style of play has led him to be described as a 'sweeper keeper'. As captain of Germany he won the 2014 World Cup and was awarded the Golden Glove for the best goalkeeper of the tournament.

FLASH FACT

Between 2013 and 2015, Manuel Neuer has won the IFFHS World's Best Goalkeeper award three years running!

David De Gea

Spanish goalkeeper David De Gea was Manchester United's Player of the Year between 2014 and 2016. In the same period he picked up every award for the Premier League Save of the Season as voted for by the *Match of the Day* TV programme. De Gea's **reflexes** are outstanding, and help him to pull off strings of impossible-looking saves.

Thibaut Courtois

Belgian goalkeeper Thibaut Courtois stands 1.99 metres high and is a daunting figure in goal for strikers to face. Courtois started playing for Chelsea in 2014 and helped them win the Premier League in his first season. In that year he kept an incredible 32 **clean sheets**. Born in 1992, Courtois still has his best years ahead of him.

Hugo Lloris

French and Tottenham Hotspur goalkeeper Hugo Lloris possesses cat-like agility and lightning reflexes. For strikers, he is considered one of the toughest keepers to face in a one-on-one situation. Like many great goalkeepers, Lloris is a commanding leader and captains both his club and country team.

WOMEN'S FOOTBALL

Women's football is growing in popularity around the world. Here are some of the best on the planet today.

Magnificent Marta

Marta from Brazil is without doubt the best female player of all time. Marta is a classic number ten, known for her creativity, flair and goalscoring. She is small and quick, yet strong and tenacious. Marta also has quick feet and remarkable skill on the ball which allows her to dribble at pace. Between 2006 and 2010 she won FIFA World Player of the Year a record five times.

FLASH FACT

Marta holds the record for the most goals scored at FIFA Women's World Cup tournaments. She has found the net 15 times.

Kim Little

Scottish midfielder Kim Little is a scoring sensation. Little is always looking to be positive and make forward runs, which puts her in positions to grab goals and make assists. Between 2008 and 2013 she helped Arsenal Ladies win five English league titles. In 2016, she was named BBC Women's Footballer of the Year.

Alex Morgan

American Alex Morgan (left) is one of the most prolific strikers in women's football. Morgan has the speed to outrun defenders and the finishing skill to outwit goalkeepers. In 2016, Morgan passed 100 caps for the United States national team and scored 17 goals in just 21 appearances.

Steph Houghton

England captain and Manchester City defender Steph Houghton (right) has made over 70 appearances for her country. In the 2012 Summer Olympics Houghton played for the Great Britain side and scored in all three group games. Her performances led her to be named the 'left back of the tournament'. Houghton has everything it takes to be a world-class defender – she can head and tackle, but also has that touch of skill and flair to play out from the back.

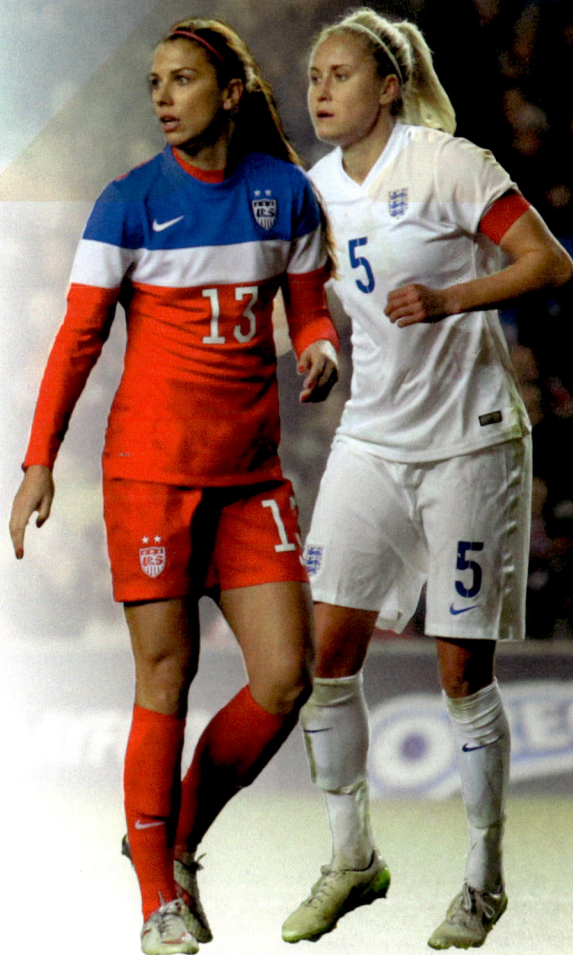

Amandine Henry

French player Amandine Henry is perhaps the best midfielder in the women's game today. In 2015, she finished second in the UEFA Best Women's Player in Europe award behind German striker Celia Sasic, who retired that year. Henry is ultra-competitive and athletic and has the ability to control football matches for her side.

Stat Tracker

	Games played	Goals
Marta Brazil	101	105
Alex Morgan USA	120	73
Amandine Henry France	48	6
Steph Houghton England	70	8
Kim Little Scotland	117	46

STARS OF THE FUTURE

These are the top young talents that have the potential to be the megastars of the future.

Man U double-act

Manchester United's future looks very bright. In Anthony Martial (right) and Marcus Rashford (left) they have two forwards who could dominate the league for years to come.

Martial was signed from French club Monaco in 2015 for a fee that could rise to £57.6 million. In the same year Martial won the Golden Boy award for the best under-21 player in Europe. He has the speed, skill and calmness in front of goal that gives defences nightmares.

Rashford is a couple of years younger than Martial but equally **dynamic** and dangerous. In 2016, aged just 18, Rashford became the youngest player ever to score on his debut for England.

Gabriel Jesus

In 2017, Manchester City signed hot prospect and Brazilian forward Gabriel Jesus for a total fee of £31 million. In 2015, Jesus had helped his club Palmeiras win the Copa do Brasil knockout cup and was voted the best newcomer in the Brazilian league. Known for his pace, finishing and work rate, Jesus sensationally scored two goals and made an assist on his Brazil debut in 2016.

Kingsley Coman

French winger Kingsley Coman is one of the most promising young players of his generation. In 2015, the Juventus player started a two-year **loan** at giants Bayern Munich. There, he won his eighth club trophy before his 20th birthday! Coman is a brilliant dribbler who has the tricks and vision to beat defenders and set up goals.

Stat Tracker

	Games played	Goals
Anthony Martial Manchester United France	69 15	23 1
Marcus Rashford Manchester United England	44 6	14 1
Gabriel Jesus Palmeiras Brazil	83 6	28 4
Kingsley Coman Bayern Munich France	44 11	6 1
Renato Sanches Bayern Munich Portugal	15 12	0 1

FLASH FACT

When wonderkid Renato Sanches (below) joined the Benfica youth system at the age of nine, his team paid €750 and 25 footballs for his signing!

Renato Sanches

Midfielder Renato Sanches has had a dream start to his football career. After winning the Portuguese league in his debut season with Benfica, Bayern Munich signed him in a deal that could total €80 million! Then, at just 18 years old, Sanches helped Portugal win Euro 2016 and was named Young Player of the Tournament. Sanches has such a wide range of skills that he can play anywhere across the midfield.

GLOSSARY

agile able to move quickly and easily

assist a pass from which a teammate scores

box-to-box midfielder an energetic midfielder who helps the team's attack and defence equally

cap appearance for the national team

centre of gravity the central part of the body from which weight takes effect

clean sheet when a goalkeeper concedes no goals in a game

commanding the ability to dominate

Copa America a major tournament contested by national sides from South America

debut first appearance for a new team

dummy a pretend kick (plural: dummies)

dynamic highly active and energetic

East Germany a former country that reunited with West Germany in 1990 to form present-day Germany

Europa League a European club competition for teams that have finished close to the top of their national league

foul an action which breaks the rules of the game, such as pushing, tripping or handball

Golden Boot an award given to the top scorer in a competition

intercept stop an opponent's pass

loan when a club borrows a player from another club for a set time

nutmeg kick the ball through the opponent's legs

one-on-one a chance for the striker to score, where they just have the goalkeeper to beat

penalty a free shot from the penalty spot (11 metres from goal) with just the goalkeeper to beat

PFA stands for the Players' Football Association, which is a union of professional footballers

possession if a team or player has control of the ball they are in possession

prolific producing many goals

reflexes quick reactions to a moving ball

set piece when the ball is kicked back into play, such as from a corner or free kick

stepover a sharp movement of the leg over the ball, instead of kicking it, to fool the defender

touchlines the lines at the sides of a football pitch

transfer when a player moves from one club to another

veteran an older, more experienced player

vision the ability to see a good pass

work rate the amount of effort a player puts in

FURTHER INFORMATION

BOOKS

EDGE: Sporting Heroes series,
Roy Apps, Franklin Watts, 2017

Greatest Players (Planet Football),
Clive Gifford, Wayland, 2017

*Messi, Superstar: His Records,
His Life, His Epic Awesomeness*,
Duo Press LLC, 2016

Stars of All Time (World Soccer Legends),
Illusi Jokulsson, Abbeville Kids, 2017

The Ultimate Fan Book series,
Carlton Books, 2017

WEBSITES

www.fourfourtwo.com/features/
On this site you can find a list of the top 100 footballers in the world today.

www.footballsgreatest.weebly.com
Find out information about the greatest footballers of all time.

www.youtube.com/watch?v=rA1102ZzprY
Video footage of 20 of the greatest footballers in history.

www.premierleague.com/players
Find out the stats for any Premier League player.

INDEX

FOOTBALL WORLD

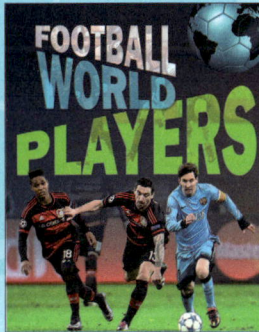

PLAYERS

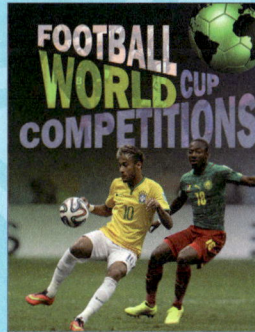

CUP COMPETITIONS

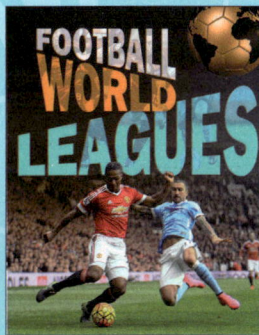

LEAGUES

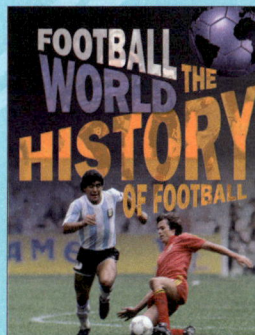

THE HISTORY OF FOOTBALL

Contents

Feast!

Long ago, most food was pretty boring. People ate bread, rice, or porridge – for every meal.

Living it up

In castles or palaces, it was a different story. Huge **feasts** were held, with meat, giant cakes, and lots more.

Boring!

Look at me!

A big castle feast wasn't just about having a nice meal. Rich people had feasts to show off to their friends or **rulers**.

Servants waited on rich people at castle feasts.

5

At the Castle

Some kings or lords threw parties in their castles and made sure the guests ate amazing food.

Roast dolphin

Castle cooks roasted birds, such as swans and herons. They even served dolphin!

Peacock was often on the menu at castle feasts.

Spicy and pricey

People ate sauces made with **spices** and fruits. These came from faraway places, so they cost a lot of money.

Peacock pie

Roman Party

The Romans loved parties. Rich people had parties with huge feasts in their houses.

Showing off

Romans served up different-sized birds that were stuffed inside each other. They liked to eat food that was hard to find, such as birds' tongues.

Tall order

I feel sick!

The Romans loved to stuff themselves full of food. Sometimes they were sick because they had eaten too much. Disgusting!

The Romans loved roasted giraffe.

9

Hot Dogs

Montezuma was a great Aztec **leader, with an amazing palace. He also loved eating!**

Turkey dinner

Montezuma ate roast turkey, snake, and dogs. Some people say the Aztecs even ate each other sometimes!

The Aztecs loved roasted snake.

Cocoa crazy

The Aztecs made the first drinking chocolate from **cocoa beans**. No sugar was added, so it didn't taste sweet like the chocolate we drink today.

Sssssss

Chinese Feast

A long time ago, an explorer **called Marco Polo went to China. He stayed with a great leader, Kublai Khan.**

Great dining room

Khan had an amazing palace – his dining hall was made of silver and gold. It was so big that thousands of people could eat there.

Kublai Khan served camel milk at his parties.

Ice cream too

In China, Marco tasted ice cream and **noodles** for the first time. He also drank horse and camel milk, served in golden cups.

Milkshake?

13

Sun King

Louis XIV was a king of France. He was such a great king that he was called the Sun King.

Eat, eat, eat

Louis held amazing feasts. People ate five **courses** – and each course had 50 different dishes.

Louis had a sweet tooth and loved to eat cakes.

To die for

Louis' cooks took their job very seriously. One even killed himself because the fish he had ordered to cook for the king was not delivered!

Fishy business

15

Viking Feast

The Vikings were scary fighters who attacked other lands, but they also loved to cook and had big feasts.

Party time

Vikings had a big feast at **harvest** time each year. They held it in a huge village house called a longhouse.

The Vikings loved parties – and fighting!

Chop, chop!

The Vikings ate with a knife only. They used it to chop up their food, then stab and grab it. They ate lots of fish, **seal**, and meat such as **boar**.

Never boaring!

Spice Kings

Great kings ruled India a long time ago. They were called Mughals, and they loved to eat spicy food.

Get stuffed!

One Mughal king's favourite food was an egg stuffed inside a small bird, stuffed inside a chicken, stuffed inside a goat, stuffed inside a camel. Phew!

Mughal palaces were filled with wonderful paintings.

Hot, hot, hot

Perfect palace

The Mughals built amazing palaces which they decorated with painted wall tiles, rugs, and beautiful paintings.

Babylon

A long time ago, people lived in a place called Babylon. They had wonderful feasts.

Left behind

We know what the people in Babylon ate because they left their recipes behind.

Boinggg!

Hopping snack

Don't miss the roasted grasshoppers! The Babylonians loved this crispy, crunchy insect. It was a favourite snack.

The Babylonians loved a crunchy grasshopper!

Glossary

Aztec people who lived in South America a long time ago

boar pig-like animal with sharp tusks

cocoa beans beans that are made into chocolate

courses stages of a meal, such as a starter, main course, and a dessert or pudding

explorer person who travels to other places to find out what they are like

feasts great parties where people eat lots of food

guests people who are invited to a party

harvest time when crops are ready to be picked

noodles a long, stringy food a little like spaghetti

porridge food made from oats mixed with water or milk

rulers people who are in charge

seal animal with flippers that lives in cold places

servants people who worked for rich rulers

spices ingredients that make food taste good

Further Reading

Websites

Find out more about what people ate in the past at:
www.historyforkids.org/learn/food/index.htm

Books

They Ate What?! The Weird History of Food
by Richard Platt, Two-Can Publishing (2006).

Food and Cooking in Roman Times
by Clive Gifford, Wayland (2009).

Food and Cooking in Viking Times
by Clive Gifford, Wayland (2009).

Index